GREAT INVENTIONS
THE WHEEL

STEWART ROSS

Text by Stewart Ross
© copyright in this edition Tulip Books 2018

The right of the Author to be identified as the Author of this work has been asserted by the Author in accordance with the Copyright, Designs and Patents Act 1988.

Every attempt has been made by the Publisher to secure appropriate permissions for material reproduced in this book. If there has been any oversight we will be happy to rectify the situation in future editions or reprints. Written submissions should be made to the Publishers.

All rights reserved.

ISBN 978-1-78388-152-9

Index

Rolling .... 4 – 5

Wheels for pots .... 6 – 7

Carts and chariots .... 8 – 9

Axels and spokes .... 10 – 11

Mill wheels .... 12 – 13

Spinning wheels .... 14 – 15

Industrial wheels .... 16 – 17

Bicycle wheels .... 18 – 19

Tyres .... 20 – 21

Fun wheels .... 22 – 23

Glossary 24

Rolling

Our world moves on wheels, but we do not know who made the first wheel.

Long ago, heavy objects were rolled on wooden logs. That's how enormous stones were **transported** many kilometres to **Stonehenge.**

WOW!
Stonehenge's 25-ton stones were brought 32 km on rollers.

Wheels for pots

Wheels were invented in the city of **Ur** about 5,500 years ago.

They were used for making pots.

Potters shaped clay and placed it on a heavy stone wheel that span round.

I NEVER KNEW!

Before the invention of the wheel, pots were made from coils of clay.

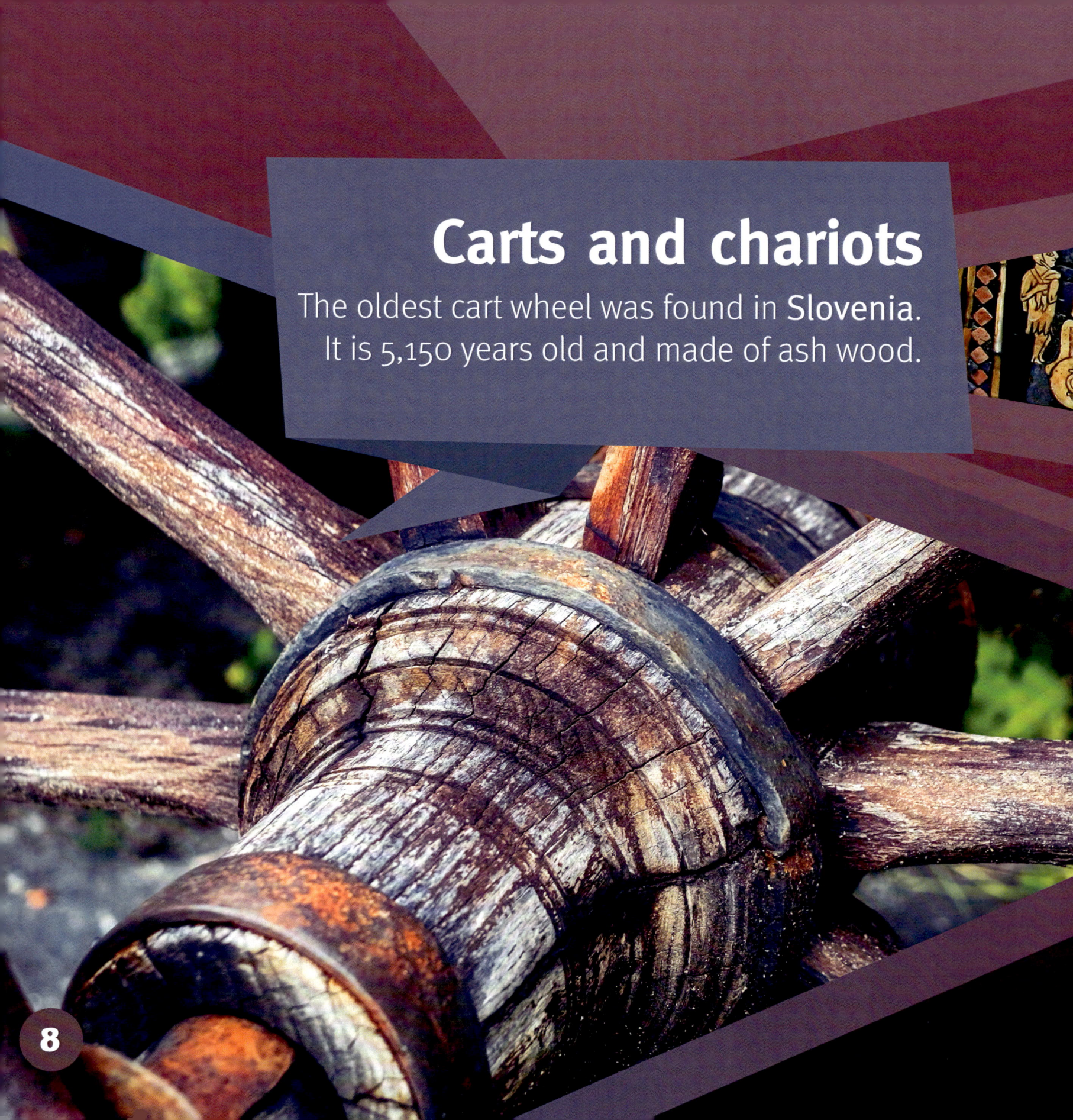

Carts and chariots

The oldest cart wheel was found in **Slovenia**. It is 5,150 years old and made of ash wood.

By 2500 BCE, the people of **Sumer** were driving war **chariots** with four solid wooden wheels.

I NEVER KNEW!

The battle chariots of Ur were pulled by wild **asses**, known as *onagers*.

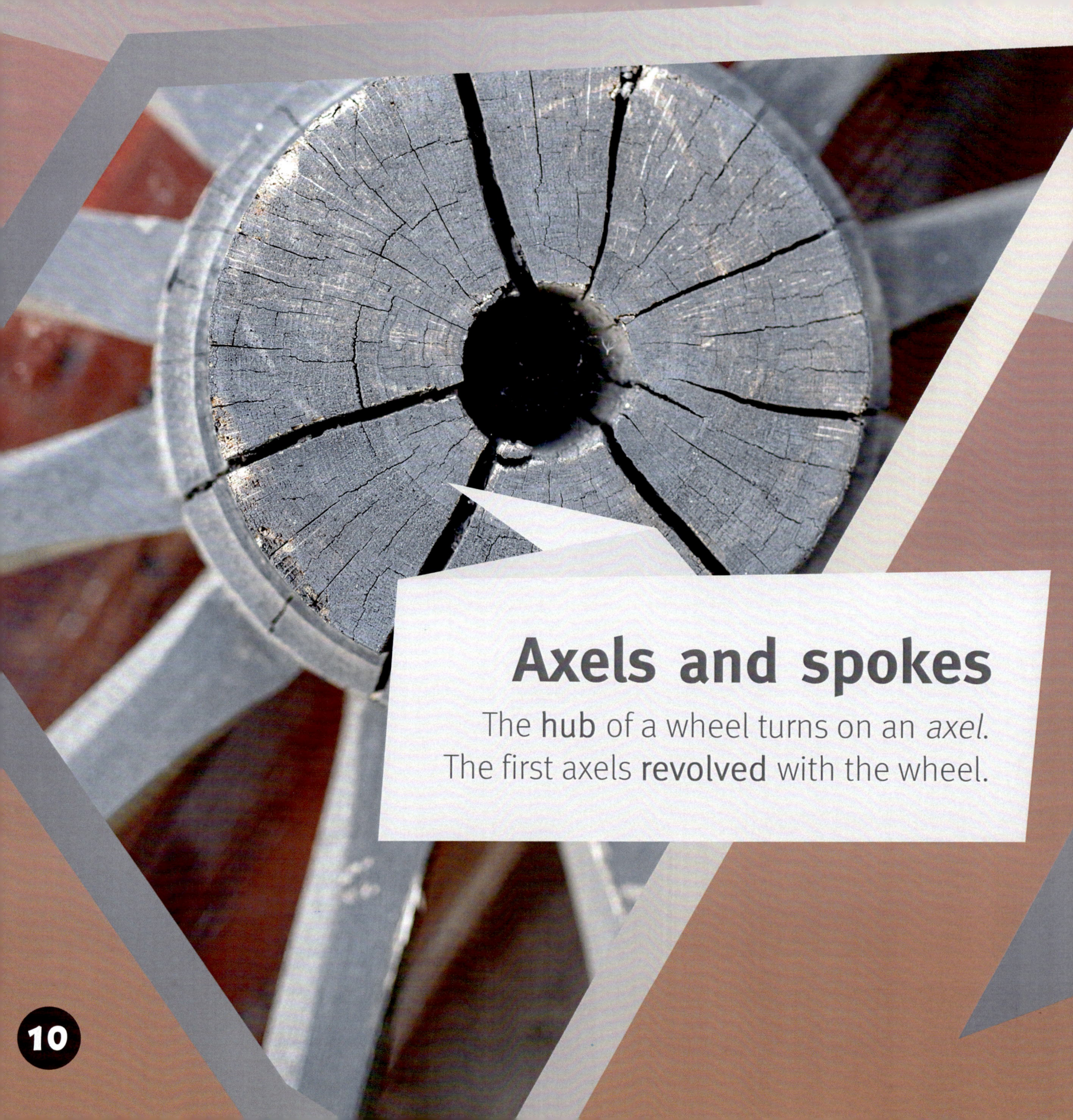

Axels and spokes
The **hub** of a wheel turns on an *axel*. The first axels **revolved** with the wheel.

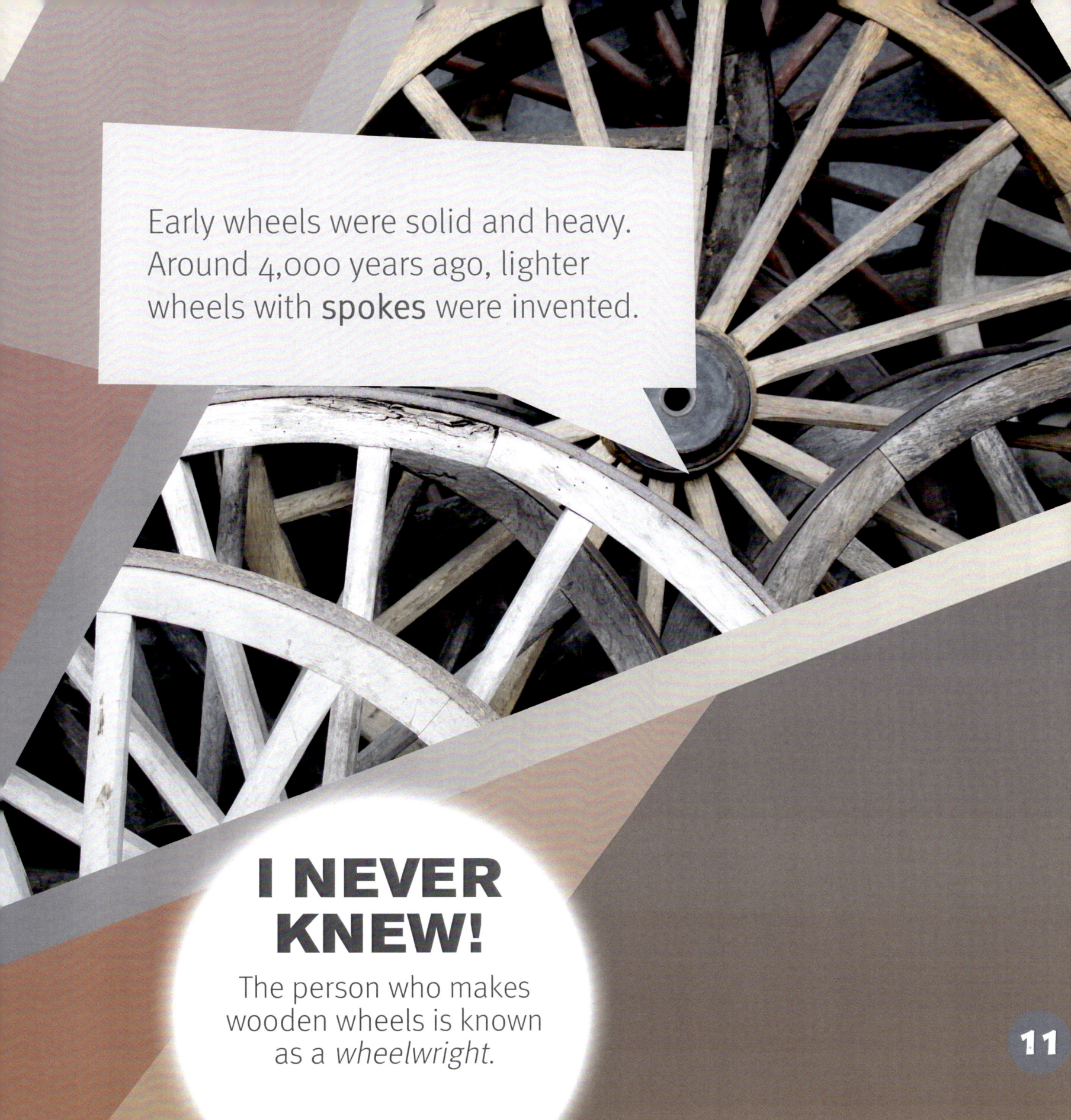

Early wheels were solid and heavy. Around 4,000 years ago, lighter wheels with **spokes** were invented.

I NEVER KNEW!

The person who makes wooden wheels is known as a *wheelwright*.

Mill wheels
Wheels were used to grind corn as well as make pots.

The corn was ground to **flour** between large stone mill wheels.

These were turned by water wheels or the sails of a windmill.

WOW!

A river turns a water wheel either by falling on it from above or by pushing it at the bottom.

Spinning wheels
In the Middle Ages, cloth was made at home by **spinning** and **weaving**.

Many homes had a *spinning wheel* (invented about 700 CE). It twisted (*spun*) loose material, like wool or silk, into thread.

I NEVER KNEW!

Spinning was done mostly by women, which is why an unmarried woman is known as a 'spinster'!

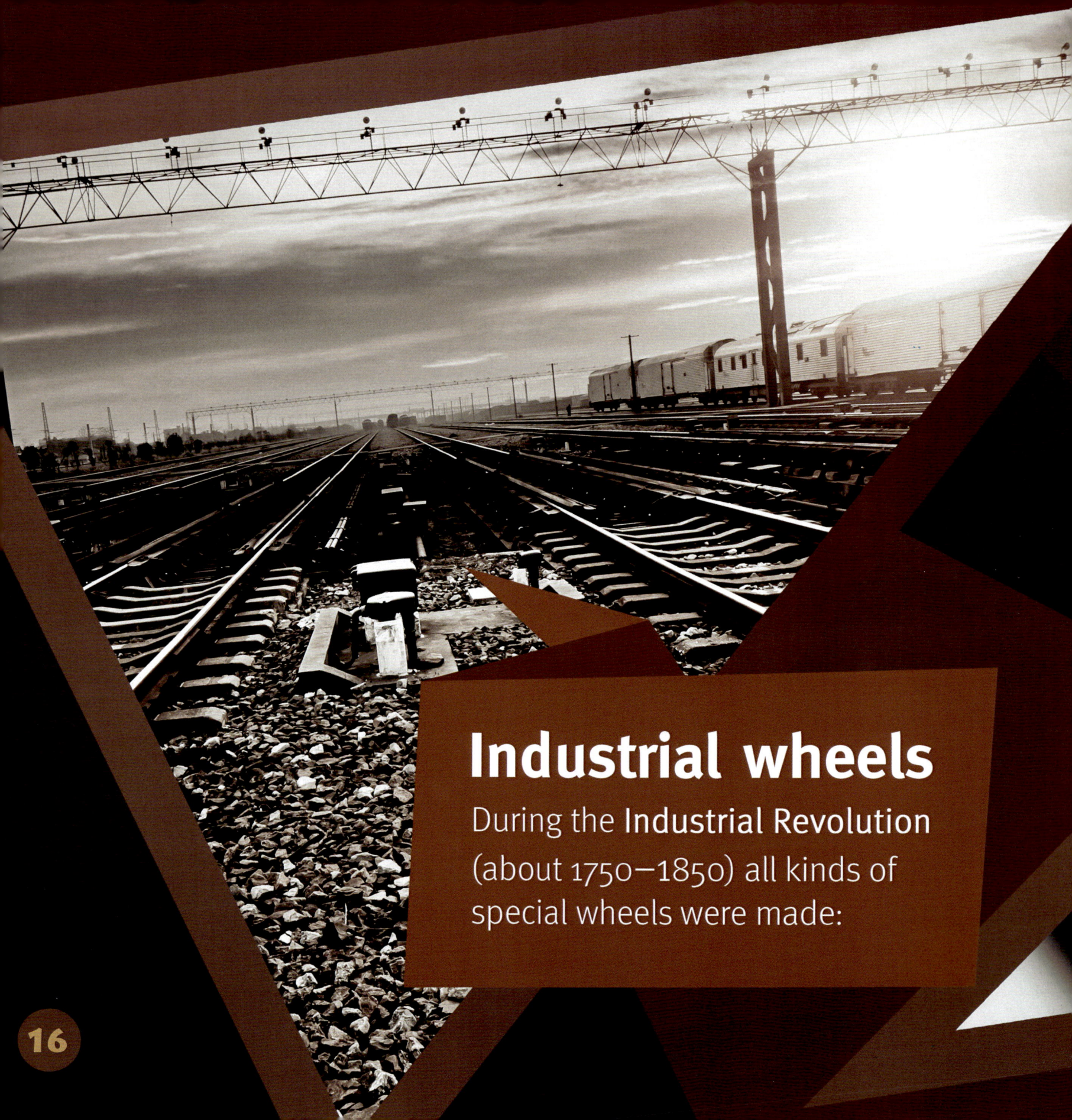

Industrial wheels

During the Industrial Revolution (about 1750–1850) all kinds of special wheels were made:

tiny wheels for watches, steel wheels for railways, **cog wheels** for machines, and **cranks** for engines.

I NEVER KNEW!

Steam engines need a heavy **fly wheel** to run smoothly.

Bicycle wheels

Spokes hold the **rim** of a wheel in place. In the 19th century, wire spokes were invented. They work by pulling the rim inwards.

Wire spokes make wheels light and strong – ideal for bicycles!

WOW!

Not surprisingly, an early bicycle with wooden wheels and iron tyres was known as a *boneshaker*!

Tyres

The first tyres were made of solid leather, iron or rubber. They were noisy and uncomfortable to ride on.

In 1888, John Dunlop invented a *pneumatic* (filled with air) tyre. Nowadays, nearly all tyres pneumatic.

I NEVER KNEW!

Dunlop invented the pneumatic tyre because his son got headaches while riding a tricycle with solid tyres!

Fun wheels

Wheels are all around us:
on the road, in the air and on the sea.
We couldn't do without them.

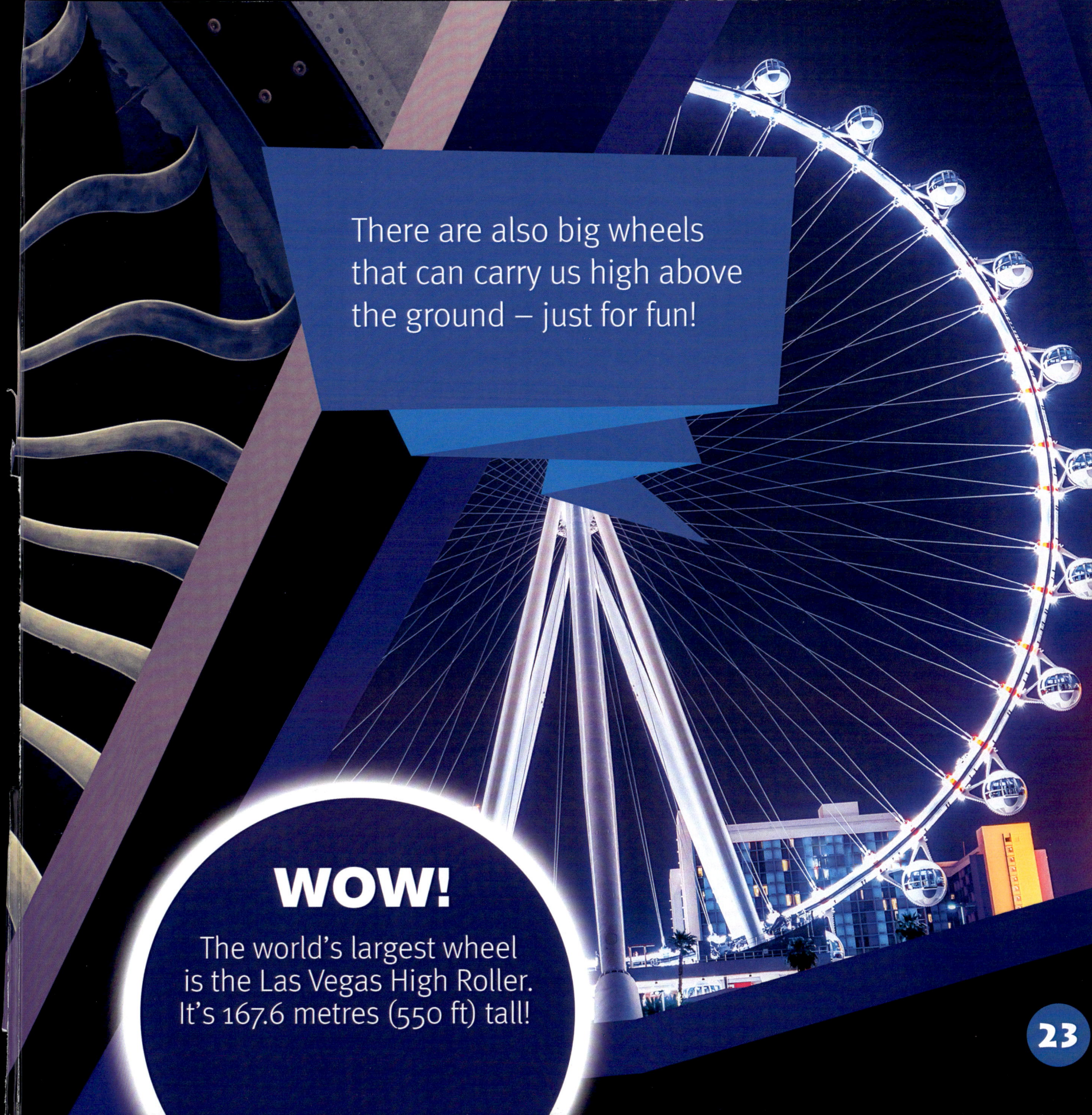

There are also big wheels that can carry us high above the ground – just for fun!

WOW!

The world's largest wheel is the Las Vegas High Roller. It's 167.6 metres (550 ft) tall!

Glossary

Ass
A donkey.

Chariot
A battle wagon pulled by horses or oxen.

Cog wheel
A wheel with teeth that can grip other cog wheels.

Crank
A device that changes up and down movement into circular movement, and vice versa.

Flour
A powder made from ground corn, used to make bread and cakes.

Fly wheel
A heavy wheel that makes the jerky movement of an engine smooth.

Grind
To crush into small pieces.

Hub
The centre of a wheel.

Industrial Revolution
The time when countries began making things with machines in factories.

Revolve
To turn round.

Rim
The outer edge of a wheel.

Slovenia
A small country in eastern Europe.

Spin
To twist a material, like wool, into thread.

Spokes
Strands of metal or wood that link the hub of a wheel to the rim.

Stonehenge
An ancient monument in southern Britain.

Sumer
A land (modern-day Iraq) where human civilization began.

Transport
To carry from one place to another.

Ur
A city of ancient Sumer.

Weave
To make cloth by criss-crossing lots of threads.